THE LORD YOUR HEALER

Colin Dye

Dovewell Publications

Dovewell Publications
Kensington Temple
Kensington Park Road
London
W11 3BY
England

Scriptural quotations are from the New King James Version,
Thomas Nelson Inc., 1991.

ISBN 1 898 444 95 1

Produced and printed by Gazelle Creative Productions Ltd,
Concorde House, Grenville Place, Mill Hill, London, NW7 3SA

CONTENTS

longing for healing   5

the Lord your healer   11

God wills healing   20

God earnt healing   28

God promises healing   39

God guarantees life   46

ask the Father   58

believe the promises   63

confess God's word   68

wait patiently   73

seek verification   80

testify publicly   84

healed to serve   88

biblical passages   93

'I am the LORD who heals you'

Exodus 15:26

longing for healing

ARE YOU LONGING FOR HEALING? Most people are. Some are even so desperate that they're willing to try anything, to spend any amount, to trust anyone who promises them healing.

Everywhere you go today, you'll find a great variety of people, therapies and products claiming to be able to make you better. You can hardly walk down a high street or open a magazine without noticing a 'healer' urging you to use their services and buy their products.

It's much the same in the church. The healing ministry has a higher profile than a few years ago, and sometimes it can be difficult to know where best to turn.

For example, some churches have developed special care for the elderly, the dying and people suffering from AIDS; others have trained small teams to pray privately for the sick; and many focus on large public healing meetings.

All these approaches are valuable - so long as you don't focus too much on the people doing the caring or praying, and don't think that you can be healed only when 'they' minister to you.

It's important you remember the basic biblical principle that the anointing for healing rests on JESUS. God wants you to learn to look to HIM for healing. You don't have to wait for someone else to pray, you can go directly to Him.

'God anointed Jesus of Nazareth with the Holy Spirit and with power, who went about doing good and healing all who were oppressed by the devil.' *Acts 10:38*

Jesus is the Christ (the word means anointed). He is 'the Anointed'; and He was anointed by the Father to heal. This is what He does. He, He is the healer. If you're longing for healing, who better to turn to than 'the Anointed'?

THE BIBLE GUARANTEES that 'Jesus Christ is the same yesterday, today and forever'. This means that His anointing for healing is as great today as in the days of the Bible. What He did to the sick then, He's still doing now.

So, if you're seeking healing for yourself or a loved one, go quickly to Jesus the Anointed - for He is the Lord, the Lord your healer.

Of course, when you do turn to Jesus and ask Him to heal, He may sometimes direct you to a praying member of His body. However, your focus at all times should be entirely on Him, and your trust and confidence should be placed in Him - and not in His human servants.

ACTS 10:38 IS AN IMPORTANT VERSE. Not only does it reveal Jesus' anointing to heal, it also exposes the source of all sickness. It shows you that disease, suffering and sickness come from the devil, and not from the holy God.

Remember, God is good, He heals the sick. He doesn't make people ill or cause them to suffer.

Ask yourself these easy questions. Did Jesus tell people to receive the gift of a disease from God? Did He tell the healthy to take to their beds and become ill? Did people ever become sick through His ministry?

No! He healed the sick and gave them His strength.

Of course, God can use sickness and suffering for His greater purposes. It's how He dealt with Pharaoh and it's how He taught Job.

But sickness and suffering don't come from inside God's holy nature. Instead, they're demonic, devilish things which are a terrible consequence of the first human sin.

God didn't create disease; He didn't plan sickness. He 'allowed' them - that's a quite different matter. And He's as committed to ending them as He is to ending sin.

A few people think that God's Genesis 2 curse means He created pain and suffering, but we don't know precisely how this curse operated. It may be that God handed humanity over to the evil which had begun to work through sin.

We do know, however, that when God, in judgement, subjected the world to futility, He did it in hope - He planned to reverse it. He began this reversal in Christ; and, on the last day, He will reverse it completely.

JESUS CAME TO BRIDGE THE GAP between humanity and God. On the cross, His sacrificial death made it possible for you to enjoy an intimate, personal, eternal, face-to-face relationship with the Father.

Healing is part of this relationship. When you go to God in prayer, you go to a good Father who wills good things for His people, gives good gifts to His children, and delights to heal you.

Because of the cross, you don't need someone to come between you and God for anything - you can go to Him yourself about everything.

You can ask God to forgive you, to bless you, to heal you - and, because He's a good God, He will minister to you from the depths of His love.

You don't need to wait for a Sunday service or the mid-week prayer meeting. You don't need to wait for a famous preacher to come to town. You simply need to ask God to act according to His nature – to be who He's said He is, to be the Lord your healer.

the Lord your healer

DO YOU REALLY KNOW that God is your healer? Many believers don't. They are quick to trust God as their Saviour, but slow to rely on Him as their Healer.

Yet God has made it clear in the Scriptures that He is both a saving and a healing God.

In Exodus 15:26, for example, He personally introduced Himself to the people of Israel as 'Yahweh Rapha', as 'the Lord who heals you'.

It was a special moment. God had just acted as their Saviour by saving them from slavery in

Egypt and danger at the Red Sea. Then, as they began their long journey to the Promised Land, He explained that He was their healer too.

Everything that follows in the Old Testament is based on this revelation that the God who had saved His people from slavery would also heal them from sickness.

The books of Leviticus and Deuteronomy contain a host of practical guidelines from God for the good health of the children of Israel.

1 & 2 Kings record how God often intervened to bring healing through the prophets.

Even the existence of Israel as a nation was down to God's healing of Sarah's barrenness! It's little wonder that King David proclaimed:

'This is the Lord who forgives all your iniquities, who heals all your diseases.'
Psalm 103:3

Do you see the wonderful balance in this statement? David knew from his experience that forgiveness is fundamental, that it's the number one item on God's agenda.

But forgiveness is not the only item on God's agenda. King David affirmed that God forgives every sin and that He heals every disease.

If sinful David knew this long before the cross, how much more should you know it today!

IT'S A SIMILAR STORY in the New Testament. At the beginning of His ministry to Israel, Jesus announced in the Nazareth synagogue:

'The Spirit of the Lord is upon Me because He has anointed Me to preach the gospel to the poor. He has sent Me to heal the broken-hearted, to preach deliverance to the captives and recovery of sight to the blind, to set at liberty those who are oppressed.' *Luke 4:18*

It was an important moment. Jesus had just been introduced by John the Baptist as 'the Lamb of God who takes away the sins of the world'; He had just passed through the waters of baptism; and He had just returned victoriously from an encounter in the wilderness with His enemy.

And here Jesus reveals publicly that He has been anointed with the Spirit and 'sent to heal'.

Everything that follows in the Gospels is based on this revelation that the One who takes away sin also takes away sickness, that the anointing also means healing.

ALL FOUR GOSPELS are packed with examples of Jesus healing the sick – and some of the stories are very well known.

He healed a nobleman's son when the son wasn't even present. He healed Jairus' daughter when she'd been dead a short while. He healed a woman who'd wasted all her money on useless treatments. He healed those who were lame, blind, dumb, deaf and leprous.

He healed the paralysed man let down through a roof, the woman bent double in the synagogue, the lame man by the pool of Bethesda and Peter's feverish mother-in-law.

He healed a servant who'd been wounded by a sword only seconds before, and others who'd been ill for years.

He healed men, women, children, servants and relatives. He healed by the roadside, on journeys, in homes and gardens, at funerals and parties, in synagogues and the open air, anywhere and everywhere, publicly and privately, instantly and after a short delay.

Most of the time, Jesus healed when people came to Him and asked Him to cure them – or to cure one of their friends or relatives. In fact, the Gospels show that Jesus healed EVERYONE who came to Him asking for healing.

At times, Jesus even healed a few people who hadn't come and asked Him – when, for example, He was overwhelmed with compassion for someone's condition or the Spirit directed Him to a particular needy person.

Although repentance and forgiveness were always Jesus' top priority (even the people He healed and raised from the dead still had to die and face judgement) it is wrong to ignore the importance that Jesus gave to healing.

In many ways, His healing miracles then were the evidence that He could forgive sins. Just as His healing power today is also a sign that He's not dead but alive forevermore!

THE BIG QUESTION you have to answer is whether or not God has changed since the days of the Bible. What do you think?

Do you believe that the God who healed Sarah, Miriam and Hannah can still heal you and your loved ones? Are you certain that the God who cured Naaman, Jereboam, Hezekiah and Job can manage the same miracles today?

Is the God who gave the people of Israel so many detailed rules about rest, health and hygiene interested in the health of your family?

Has the anointing on Jesus to heal withered away? Or is it as great today as it was then? These are important questions.

Of course, those people who refuse to accept the biblical revelation don't actually make a scrap of difference to God's healing nature. Their disbelief can't diminish His power and willingness to heal!

However, their disbelief does usually stop them from approaching God, and from asking Him to heal them.

What a tragedy!

THE TRUTH OF THE BIBLICAL REVELATION about God's healing nature is confirmed by many things that you can see in the world.

Because God made humanity in His image, we've all received a small part of His passion for healing - it's why people everywhere are crying out for healing.

God has implanted His healing principle into all His creatures, and, as a result – despite the havoc wrought by sin – our bodies still largely heal themselves. The best that most doctors can do is to help this natural healing process.

Think about the number of times that you've got better when you've been ill or injured. Where do you think this healing process came from? Who made you in this wonderful way? The Lord your healer, that's who!

IT'S THE SAME IN THE CHURCH. If God has always been making His people more and more like Jesus, we should always be able to see His healing nature flowing through His church.

And that's what you can see, right through the centuries. The church has always prayed for the sick and cared for the ill and dying. It's always been believers who've started hospitals and hospices, who've pioneered and developed basic medical care, who've risked their lives in times of plague and epidemic.

Why have believers done this? It's simple. It's because they've been filled with God's healing nature. It's because they know that they serve Yahweh Rapha, the Lord who heals.

God is willing

THERE ARE MANY PEOPLE today who believe that God possesses the power to heal them, but who are far from convinced that He's willing to heal them or their loved ones.

They believe that God could heal today, if He really wanted to. But they also believe that He doesn't choose to heal very often. For them, God is 'The Lord, your reluctant healer'.

Once you're convinced that God can heal you, the next question you need to consider is whether God is willing to heal you. Well, is He? Ask yourself some more simple questions.

As God has implanted an automatic self-healing principle in His creatures, doesn't this suggest that He's automatically willing to heal you and your loved ones?

Doesn't the fact that, throughout your life, your cuts have healed and your coughs and colds have mended, say something about God's unlimited willingness to heal you?

If God has filled His world with plants and remedies which facilitate healing, doesn't this suggest that He wants you to be healed?

Doesn't the fact, that Jesus healed EVERYONE who came to Him seeking healing, challenge the idea that He's reluctant to heal people?

As God has introduced Himself as the healer, would He still be a good God if He could heal His people but was unwilling to heal them?

Sometimes we don't think hard enough. If God is a good God (and He is, He is) He must be filled with an overwhelming willingness to heal people, to heal you, to heal your loved ones. Nothing else makes any sense!

MARK'S GOSPEL BEGINS with a typical day in the life of Jesus.

In 1:21-39, Mark describes how Jesus taught in a synagogue, cast out an evil spirit, astonished people with His authority, healed Simon Peter's mother-in-law, and then healed 'many who were sick with various diseases'.

The word was out about Jesus' healing power. The sick of Galilee were flocking to find Him. Everyone wanted to meet Him.

Mark then tells a moving story. In 1:40-45, Mark describes how a man riddled with leprosy risked everything by approaching Jesus.

Under the Jewish law, lepers weren't allowed this sort of contact with people. They had to carry a bell and wear special clothes to identify themselves. They even had to cry, 'Unclean, unclean,' whenever they saw anyone.

The man who came to Jesus was disfigured with leprosy, socially isolated, and used to telling people to keep out of his way. He'd never dared to approach anyone like this before.

The scarred, rejected leper knew that Jesus had the power to heal him, but he wasn't sure whether Jesus would be willing to heal someone like him. Does he sound familiar?

WHAT HAPPENS NEXT IS CRITICAL. What Jesus didn't say and what He did say are equally significant.

Jesus didn't ask the man to wait while He checked with God whether the man was lucky enough to be on God's list for healing.

Jesus didn't praise the man for his boldness, then warn him not to be disappointed. And He didn't explain that God only healed on very special occasions.

Jesus didn't say that most people weren't healed, and that he was probably one of them. And He didn't remind the man that healing wasn't for everyone, but that he could have a different blessing instead!

The leper had gasped, 'If You are willing, You can make me clean'. Mark 1:41 describes Jesus' quick response.

'And Jesus, moved with compassion, put out His hand and touched him, and said to him, "I am willing; be cleansed."'

When the man asked Jesus whether He was willing, Jesus didn't need to check with His Father for further instructions.

He knew immediately, without any doubts or qualifications, that God is filled with an unqualified, unlimited willingness to heal. It's fundamental to His perfectly good nature.

24

THERE'S MORE! Did you notice that Jesus touched the man? What a risk! What compassion!

Jesus didn't heal the leper from a safe distance, He touched him - something nobody had done since he became ill. Can you imagine what this must have meant to the man?

And Jesus didn't heal the man to prove anything about Himself. He didn't do it to show off, or to advertise His ministry, or to demonstrate that He was the Son of God.

Instead, Jesus healed the man because He was filled with the Father's compassion, with the Father's perfect goodness, with the Father's unlimited willingness to heal.

Jesus is still the same today. He's still filled with the same compassion, still filled with the same willingness to heal, still filled with the same power to heal. He has not changed.

Indeed, because Jesus is the eternal God, He cannot change.

THE STORY OF JESUS' willingness sets the tone for the rest of the Gospel. It's a thread which runs through everything. Jesus is willing to heal, to provide, to forgive, to suffer and die, to serve hurting people in every way that they need.

So, if you're longing for healing, understand this from the very beginning. God's will is for healing. God's will for your life is healing. Jesus is willing and able to heal you. Hold on to this truth. Never doubt it.

Of course, this doesn't mean that everybody receives healing - just as not everybody receives salvation. So much is mystery.

But the deep truth you can hang onto is that God is eternally willing to heal.

Jesus never doubted this. He always ministered in total confidence of the Father's willingness to heal, and He always represented the true nature of His healing Father.

This means that, whenever you approach the Lord your healer, whether for yourself or a friend or relative, you can draw near to Him with total confidence, sure of a smile, a gentle touch and a willing response.

Remember, He's a good God, He's the Lord your healer.

God earnt healing

THERE'S ANOTHER BIG REASON why you can be certain that the Lord is your healer, and be sure that He's willing to heal you.

It's the cross.

Some people doubt that God is a healer. They ask, 'If He's all-good and all-powerful, why hasn't He dealt with all the sickness in the world?' They argue that the presence of disease proves that God must be either bad or weak.

When people reason like this, they're ignoring the cross.

You've already seen that God did not create evil, pain, suffering, death, sickness, corruption, pollution, and so on. They came into being as a result of the first human sin.

God could have made a world where sin and sickness were impossible, but only by making puppets rather than people.

In making the first man and woman free to enjoy a wonderful, face-to-face relationship with Himself, God had to make them free to reject Him and to follow their own paths.

The possibility of sin was the price of their free will. The consequences of sin are the result of their rejection of God's perfect will.

However, even while God was justly subjecting the world to futility, He was also promising that the Seed would triumph over the Serpent, that Christ would overcome evil, that Jesus would defeat Satan.

Which is exactly what happened on the cross!

In Christ, on the cross, God did EVERYTHING to deal with the root of evil - sin - and to deal with the fruit of evil – which includes guilt, death and sickness.

DO YOU REALISE just how much God accomplished for you on the cross?

On the cross, in Christ, God broke the power of evil and death so that you can be released from the grip of evil and the fear of death.

In Christ, He bore His own just wrath against sin so that you can receive His unconditional forgiveness and be clothed in His righteousness.

In Christ, He showed you how to live and die, how to handle abuse and suffering, how to deal with pain and mortality, so that you can follow Him and draw strength from His example.

On the cross, in Christ, He travailed to give birth to a new nation, to 'see His offspring', so that you can live with the new life of God within you as a genuine child of God.

IT WILL TAKE YOU ETERNITY to discover and experience the fullness of everything that God accomplished for you on-and-through the cross.

In this little book, however, you need to grasp just one aspect of His achievement. (You must always remember that it is only one aspect.)

On the cross, Satan provoked Jesus through torture, pain, lies and insults. But Jesus refused to retaliate. Instead of overcoming evil with its own weapon of force, Jesus conquered it with godly submission and perfect obedience.

Satan did everything he could to tempt Jesus to disobey God, to hate His enemies, to flinch from death. But, by His perfect obedience and love, Jesus won the decisive victory over evil.

When Jesus died without sin, Satan had to concede defeat. By His death on the cross,

Jesus achieved the critical victory over evil, and over every form and every fruit of evil - including sickness and death.

It's really very simple to understand. On the cross, Jesus died for sin. He paid the price for sin. He suffered all the consequences of sin. He broke the power of sin. He defeated sin.

This means that you can be free from sin and free from all the consequences of sin. You can be free from wickedness, free from guilt, free from hell, free from death, free from sickness!

And every aspect of your perfect freedom was earnt for you by God-in-Christ on the cross!

THE APOSTLE PETER sets this out in the second chapter of his first letter to the church.

Peter explains that 'Christ also suffered for us, leaving us an example, that you should follow His steps'.

Peter affirms that Christ 'committed no sin,

nor was any guile found in His mouth; who, when He was reviled, did not revile in return; when He suffered, He did not threaten, but committed Himself to Him who judges righteously'.

He declares that, 'Christ himself bore our sins in His own body on the tree that we, having died to sins, might live for righteousness'.

And then the apostle concludes:

'by whose stripes you were healed'.
1 Peter 2:24

Although Peter is writing mainly about forgiveness, it's clear that this conclusion is as much about healing from sickness as it is about forgiveness from sin.

If Jesus dealt with the root of evil, He also dealt with the fruit of evil. If He delivered you from sin on the cross, He also delivered you from sickness and death on the cross.

It's really true! Christ's death guarantees your healing. Sickness has been banished because sin has been vanquished. The power of death and disease has been broken, because the devil has been defeated.

This is a basic spiritual reality which should transform the way that you approach God and think about healing.

YOU MUST NOT FORGET, however, that you didn't experience all the benefits of the cross fully and completely the moment that you first believed.

Christ's death guarantees every aspect of your salvation for eternity, but there is much for God to complete on the last day of resurrection.

For example, no matter how close you live to God in loving obedience, you will not reach absolute perfection and unceasing victory in this life. Satan may have been decisively defeated on the cross, but he has not yet been fully destroyed and finally eliminated.

Instead, your increasing holiness is a wonderful foretaste of your certain eternal perfection. And your every experience of victory points to the absolute triumph of the last day.

It's the same with healing. Because of the cross, you have a wonderful inheritance of healing. But it is essentially incomplete in this life – you know that not everyone is healed of everything and that everyone who is healed eventually dies.

However, every healing that you experience is a foretaste of the ultimate release you will experience at the last day of resurrection. And every healing you receive points prophetically forward to the great and wonderful day when 'there will be no more pain'.

Every time you turn to 'The Lord your healer', you celebrate the decisive healing breakthrough of the cross. You show that you're living in the good of this important blessing, and are applying it in your life.

But don't forget that your total healing will not be finally and fully completed until the last day of resurrection. After that, you'll never need healing again!

JESUS' HEALING MINISTRY on the cross is the fulfilment of Isaiah's 700 year-old prophecy:

'He has borne our griefs (or sicknesses) and carried our sorrows (or pain); yet we esteemed Him stricken, smitten by God and afflicted. But He was wounded for our transgressions, He was bruised for our iniquities; the chastisement for our peace was upon Him, and by His stripes we are healed.' *Isaiah 53:4-5*

This is a wonderful prophecy that the bearing of sickness and pain will take place on the cross. Memorise this verse, and let it remind you that

Jesus came to relieve you of your burdens of sin, sickness and pain, that His wounds really do make you whole.

SOME BELIEVERS, when they read Isaiah's prophecy, wonder how Jesus managed to heal anyone before the cross.

The answer is easy. Jesus healed before the cross in the same way that He forgave people before the cross - and in the same way that God had been forgiving and healing Israel for a thousand years before the cross.

First, God gave healing and forgiveness to people before the cross on the basis of what He was going to do for them on the cross. He healed and forgave them on credit!

Second, every part of Jesus' earthly life was deeply inter-related with His death. His life wasn't one thing and His death something different. The way that Jesus triumphed over sickness and sin in His earthly life paved the way for His decisive defeat of death and sickness on the cross.

Isaiah's prophecy should make it impossible for you ever to separate healing from Christ's finished work on the cross.

It establishes that, by bearing your sin, Jesus bore your sickness; that, by taking your guilt, He incurred your punishment, and that your total healing came at the cost of His terrible wounds.

It's true, by His stripes, you were healed!

God promises healing

YOU'VE GRASPED THAT THE BIBLE reveals God to be the healing God, that it recounts the healing miracles He has worked, and that it records the ultimate healing of the cross.

Now there's more, for the Bible also contains many promises of healing and prayers for healing which you can read, learn, claim, confess and use.

Christian believers have always rightly relied on God's promises to fill them with hope for this life and the life to come.

For example, through the Bible you can be reassured that your heavenly Father knows you intimately (even the hairs on your head are numbered), that He cares about you deeply, and that He'll provide you with all the necessities of life.

When you despair about making ends meet, the promises of God's Word will give you strength to keep going in hope.

And, for example, you know that Jesus will return for His bride and fully establish His kingdom only because you've read and believed the relevant promises in God's Word.

So, when you despair about the deteriorating state of the world, the Bible promises help you to see beyond your concerns and recognise that God is in ultimate control - working everything out according to His purposes

It's much the same with healing. When you're worried by the condition of a loved one, or by your own pain, the promises of God's Word can bring tremendous hope, assurance and comfort. But only if you know them and use them!

HERE ARE SOME of the healing promises contained in God's Word. Read them. Meditate upon them. Memorise them. Claim them. Allow them to sink deep into your spirit. Confess their truth with your lips. Return to them again and again. Allow God to speak to you through them.

'I am the Lord who heals you.' *Exodus 15:26*

'God will wipe away every tear from their eyes; there shall be no more death, nor sorrow nor crying: and there shall be no more pain, for the former things have passed away.'
Revelation 21:4

'As many as touched Him were made well.'
Mark 6:56

'Bless the Lord, O my soul, and forget not all His benefits; who forgives your iniquities, who heals all your diseases, who redeems you from destruction.' *Psalm 103:3-4*

'Fear the Lord and depart from evil. It will be health to your flesh and strength to your bones.'
Proverbs 3:7-8

'They brought to Him all sick people who were afflicted with various diseases and torments, and those who were demon-possessed, epileptics and paralytics; and He healed them.'
Matthew 4:24

'The Lord will strengthen him on his bed of illness; You will sustain him on his sick-bed.'
Psalm 41:3

'He sent His word and healed them.'
Psalm 107:20

'The Lord binds up the bruise of His people and heals the stroke of their wound.' *Isaiah 30:26*

'A multitude gathered from the surrounding cities, bringing sick people and those who were tormented by evil spirits and they were all healed.' *Acts 5:16*

'"I will restore health to you and heal you of your wounds" says the Lord.' *Jeremiah 30:17*

'Come, and let us return to the Lord, for He has torn, but He will heal us. He has stricken, but He will bind us up.' *Hosea 6:1*

'Your healing shall spring forth speedily.'
Isaiah 58:8

'I have seen his ways and will heal him. I will also lead him, and restore comforts to him.'
Isaiah 57:18

'Great multitudes followed Him, and He healed them.' *Matthew 19:2*

'To you who fear My name, the Sun of Righteousness shall arise with healing in His wings.' *Malachi 4:2*

'The blind receive their sight and the lame walk; the lepers are cleansed and the deaf hear; the dead are raised up...' *Matthew 11:5*

'Many who were paralysed and lame were healed.' *Acts 8:7*

'He who raised Christ from the dead will also give life to your mortal bodies through His Spirit who dwells in you.' *Romans 8:11*

'He showed me a pure river of the water of life, clear as crystal, proceeding from the throne of God and the Lamb. In the middle of its street, and on either side of the river, was the tree of life, which bore twelve fruits, each tree yielding its fruit every month. And the leaves of the tree were for the healing of the nations.'
Revelation 22:1-2

TREASURE THESE PRECIOUS PROMISES. They are God's Word; they are true and reliable; they carry His personal guarantee. What He has promised, He will do. What He has done before, He will do again, for He is the Lord your healer.

God guarantees life

THE GOSPELS MAKE IT CLEAR that Jesus healed everybody who came to Him requesting healing, and that He healed many more to whom God sent Him directly.

Wherever you turn in the Gospels, you'll see convincing evidence of Jesus' unlimited power and willingness to heal. However, you mustn't overlook the fact that Jesus did not heal all the sick people in Israel.

For example, when Jesus healed the lame man at the pool of Bethesda, it seems that He didn't heal any of the other sick people who were lying round the pool at the time.

And although Jesus must have often passed the crippled man who lay at the Temple gate called Beautiful, the man had to wait until after Pentecost for his miraculous healing.

IT'S A SIMILAR STORY in the rest of the New Testament.

When you read the book of Acts, you'll see many examples of wonderful healing miracles - the crippled man at the temple, Paul (twice), Aeneas, Tabitha, Eutychus, Publius' father, a lame man at Lystra, and so on.

The book of Acts also makes it clear that healing miracles were a significant part of the life and mission of the disciples, and one of the key reasons for the rapid growth of the church.

Crowds flocked to the Christian community for healing. The apostles ministered to EVERYONE who came requesting healing. And 'unknown' disciples like Ananias were quick to respond to the Spirit's leading to take God's healing to others - even to an enemy of the church.

Acts is a wonderful testimony to God's power and willingness to heal people in this life. Paul's letters, however, reveal that not everyone was healed 'on the spot' in New Testament days.

Paul reported, for example, that he'd had to leave one of his ministry team behind in Miletus because he was sick. He advised one of his assistants to start drinking a little wine to ease his frequent stomach infirmities.

And there are indications in a few of his letters that Paul himself may have suffered at times from a troubling eye condition.

THIS MIXTURE OF MIRACLES and mystery is similar to the experience of most Spirit-filled believers and churches today.

The reality we face is that some people are healed when we do not expect them to be, and that others are not healed when we feel sure that they will be.

If you haven't experienced both these puzzling mysteries yet, you will do soon!

On the one hand there is overwhelming evidence of God's power to heal today, of God's willingness to heal today, and of God's promises to heal today.

On the other hand, the plain fact is that not everybody was immediately healed in the New Testament and that not everyone is healed today.

It's a mystery, and you have to live in the tension of this mystery. It's no good pretending that everyone gets healed, and it's dishonest to suggest that God doesn't heal today.

You just have to embrace the mystery and stand firm on God's revelation and promises.

WHEN YOU START TO PRAY for healing – no matter whether for yourself or for others – you'll have to grapple hard with the mystery.

You'll be faced with some people who are not healed, with others whose initial healing lapses, and with a few who start to improve and then make no more progress.

Everyone handles these situations differently. Some believers put all the blame on the devil. Others insist that it's due to sin in the life of the person seeking healing. A few think it can be explained by a lack of faith. But these are rarely the truth.

Sometimes the lack of healing is our fault. We can mishear God. We can be impatient or over-enthusiastic. We can be bound by a tradition or fascinated by a phenomena. We can give up after a set-back or simply be out of our depth.

But the devil will try to convince you that it is always your fault – and that will be completely untrue. It's simply a mystery which nobody can explain.

God has made it clear that it is His will to heal everyone – just as it is His will to save everyone. But not everyone gets healed – just as not everyone gets saved.

It's a real head-scratching, mind-puzzling mystery! And you've got to wait for heaven to learn the answer.

MEANWHILE, GOD HASN'T LEFT YOU to flounder with embarrassment at a lack of healing, because there is so much that you can guarantee to someone who's not healed.

Because of Christ's death on the cross, every believer can look forward to a new and perfect body at the day of resurrection. This means that you can look every sick believer straight in the eye and promise them that they will be wonderfully healed.

You can give them an unconditional guarantee that their pain and suffering will stop, and that their frail body will be utterly transformed.

You will not know when they will be healed; but you will know for certain that it is God's will for them to be healed - and that they really will be healed!

Because of the cross, there is unlimited hope for healing for every believer in Christ. And this hope is so great and so wonderful that you should encourage every believer to embrace its every element.

Some might not be healed now in the way that you hope. But you can be 100% sure that – in Christ and because of the cross – they will be.

THE GUARANTEE OF NEW LIFE and a perfect body at the resurrection isn't a convenient excuse for those times when people are not healed in this life.

Instead, it's a scriptural principle which will help you to live with biblical hope in a world which is still groaning from its bondage of corruption.

The apostle Paul writes about exactly this hope in his letter to the church at Rome. In chapter 8, Paul promises resurrection to those in whom the Spirit dwells, explains that this involves waiting with perseverance, and promises that the sufferings of this life are not worth comparing with the glory which will be revealed in us.

Paul did not write like this to explain away an absence of healing - for the Bible records that Paul was twice healed miraculously and that healing was a vital part of his ministry.

Instead, Paul wrote like this because he was setting down an important truth. It's a truth which relates directly to the everyday experience of all Spirit-filled believers; and it's a truth which should enable you to rejoice with those who are delighting in their healing now AND to persevere with those who are waiting for their healing – either later in this life or at the last day.

ALTHOUGH YOU SHOULD always urge people to turn to the healing God, you need to be careful how you do this.

There are plenty of people about who are 'casualties' of unhelpful ministry and teaching, and you'll want to help them, not add to them!

Some believers have become cynical about healing after hearing false claims. Others have grown suspicious through being taught that God does not heal today. And a few have been brow-beaten by over-enthusiastic saints.

Some people are hurt because they've been told that their personal lack of healing is due to their own sin, or to their lack of faith, or to an insufficient desire for healing.

And many disabled people are wary of churches because of the insensitive treatment that they've received in the past.

You need to recognise that disabled people are as much in the image of God as graceful athletes, and should value the special contribution that they make in the church.

You should not assume that they are longing for healing, or that they lead unfulfilled lives. And you should try to develop an attitude which does not make them feel conspicuous, uncomfortable or unaccepted in their disability.

However, you should sensitively encourage them – as you should encourage everyone – to look to the healing anointing of Jesus.

MANY BELIEVERS HAVE TO LIVE in the tension of seeing some 'unlovable' person healed while the one that they love dearly remains unwell. At times like this, a deep understanding of the biblical principles you've considered will help you to keep things in perspective and balance.

Although you should urge people to keep on praying for their healing, and to keep claiming God's promises for healing, you should also point them to God's unconditional guarantee of new life and a perfect body at the last day.

Even more importantly, you should remind them to long more for the healer than for their healing.

Ultimately, healing is not your greatest hope. Jesus is. In the middle of this groaning world, your only hope of peace is to be found in Him - and in His grace and love.

If you're preoccupied with healing, you'll never be whole and you'll never find peace. But if God Himself is your goal, you'll find that the Lord your healer will soon embrace you in His holy healing arms.

SO FAR IN THIS LITTLE BOOK, you've been learning about the foundations of healing.

You've seen that God is a healing God, that healing is a basic part of His nature, and that - therefore - healing is part of everything He does.

You've grasped that God is not only full of infinite power to heal, but that He's also full of unlimited willingness to heal. You should have reached the point by now where you know that God can heal you and that He wills to heal you!

And you've started to read and learn the special promises about healing which are found in God's Word.

Now it's time to move on. You don't want to be someone who knows the biblical principles but never enjoys the biblical blessings!

So, for the rest of this book, you'll be learning the practical steps that you can take to receive your healing from the Lord your healer.

ask the Father

THE FIRST STEP IN RECEIVING is asking. If you don't ask, you're unlikely to receive. This isn't just a healing principle, and it isn't just a spiritual principle; it's a basic rule of life.

The apostle James wrote, 'You do not have because you do not ask'.

The much-loved hymn states, 'Oh what peace we often forfeit; Oh what needless pain we bear; all because we do not carry, everything to God in prayer'.

Even Jesus Himself promised, 'If you ask anything in My name, I will do it'.

God is willing to heal you. God is able to heal you. But you need to ask Him to heal you. You need to come before Him and make your requests known to Him in prayer.

Of course God knows what you need long before you speak, but that's no excuse for not praying. You've got to ask God for yourself because His top priority is establishing an intimate, eternal, face-to-face relationship with you which revolves around prayer.

CHRISTIAN PRAYER is mainly offered to the Father. Because of the Son's finished work on the cross, the way is now open for you to speak directly to the Father.

He is the Father of lights, and no shadow of doubt or variation ever comes from Him. He is always true to His word. He always keeps His promises. He always acts consistently with His nature. He is the good Father who gives good things to His children. In fact, EVERY good and perfect gift comes from Him, from your heavenly Father.

But Christian prayer should not only be offered 'to the Father', it must also be offered 'in Jesus' name'.

You need to ask the Father for your healing, but you need to ask Him in Jesus' name. You do this because all the Father's blessings and promises are found in Jesus' name.

THIS IS VERY IMPORTANT. The world is full of people offering healing, but they are not all from the heavenly Father.

Many of them claim that their healing comes from God, but it's easy for you to establish whether their healing comes from the Father or not. The test is simple. It's whether they heal in Jesus' name.

Healing in Jesus' name doesn't mean saying a few prayers and quoting a Scripture or two. It means being aligned with Christ; it means believing in Him alone for full salvation; it means obeying His instructions and being fully orientated towards Him.

THERE ARE ALL KINDS of so-called alternative healing practices today. They're not all bad, but many are. The best way of sifting through them is to ask yourself where the power comes from.

Many healers talk about energies and forces. They suggest that crystals will heal you and that guides will help you. This is nothing to do with healing in Jesus' name. He's a living person, not a force or energy. He heals, not a lump of rock.

Sadly, many of the 'spiritual technologies' of alternative healing are nothing more than modern forms of ancient occultism, spiritism and pagan religions.

And the issue is not whether these therapies 'work', it's who's at work.

There is much more to healing than having your physical symptoms disappear. You need to receive the life and health and wholeness of Jesus into your spirit as well as your body.

So, whenever you need healing for yourself or a loved one, turn to the Father in prayer and ask Him to heal in Jesus' name.

Jesus is the only one who has died for the sins of the whole world. He bore your griefs. He carried your sorrows. He was wounded for your transgressions. He was bruised for your iniquities. And by His stripes, you are healed.

In His name, and in His name alone, true healing flows.

believe the promises

THE PEOPLE WHO APPROACHED JESUS in the Gospels asking for healing were very clear in their beliefs.

They came to Jesus. They believed that He could heal them. They asked Him to heal them. And He healed them. It's that simple.

Their eyes were fixed on Jesus. They knew what He had done for others. They asked Him to do for them what He had done for others. And He did.

It's not complicated!

The people needed to believe in Jesus, otherwise they would not have come to Him. And they needed to believe that Jesus could heal them, otherwise they would not have bothered to ask Him for healing.

But they didn't have to work up some sort of extra-special version of five-star faith! They came. They asked. They were healed.

WHEN YOU READ the New Testament accounts of Jesus' healing ministry, and that of the early church's, you can see that the focus is not on the faith of the person coming; it's on the grace, power and willingness of Jesus to heal.

You do need faith to be healed. But you only need faith the size of a mustard seed - because it's the power and willingness of God which heals you, not anybody's faith or prayers.

Let's suppose that you've a choice between two cars for a long journey. One is a rusty old heap which has failed its road worthiness test, and the other is a brand new, chauffeur-driven Bentley.

How much faith do you need to travel in the heap? And how much faith do you need to ride in the Bentley?

Now, which of these cars is a better picture of the Lord your healer? Is He a reluctant, unreliable healer who struggles to dry up a cold? Or is He the great Maker of heaven and earth who raised Jesus from the dead and heals all diseases?

Do you see why you need faith the size of a mustard seed? Why, it's almost an insult to God to suggest that you need any more.

FAITH IS HAVING YOUR EYES fixed on God. It's reaching out to Him. It's relying on Him. It's making contact with His great power. It's believing His promises. It's saying 'Yes' to Jesus and 'Amen' to God's Word.

In fact, faith is a little bit like the clutch in a car. The car won't move unless you press the clutch, but it's the engine which is the source of all the power.

It's impossible for you to please God without faith, just as the car can't move until the driver presses the clutch. But the faith you need is nothing complicated or advanced – it's simple, trusting, childlike faith which says, 'Dear Lord, please keep Your promise, please do this.'

Do you remember the promises about healing that you read a few pages ago? Do you believe that they are God's words? Do you believe that God keeps His Word? If you do, you've all the faith you need to approach Him for healing.

FAITH COMES BY HEARING, and hearing by the Word of God, so these Bible promises are very important - as are all Jesus' words about healing and all the Bible stories of healing. At the back of this book, there's a list of the relevant Bible passages about healing. It's up to you to look them up in the Bible for yourself and read them.

When you do, you'll discover that it's a wonderful thing to dwell on Jesus' words and meditate on God's promises.

You'll find that they strengthen you, and prepare you for those times when you need to approach God for healing for yourself or a loved one.

confess God's word

GOD'S WORDS COME from the very heart of God. They originate in His mind, are empowered by His might and are energised by His Spirit.

Because of this, God's words in your mouth are as powerful as God's words in His mouth. The power is in the Word, not the speaker.

God's words are not only vested with the power and authority of God, they are also filled with His truth. When you confess His words, you speak pure truth.

Faith is not believing something which you know isn't true; it's not positive thinking; and it isn't empty confession. Instead, real faith is believing, confessing and acting on what you know to be 100% true.

This is why God's Word is so important to faith, for it is absolute truth.

A few people say, 'I'm healed', when they're plainly ill, because they've simply recited a verse of Scripture or a statement based on positive thinking. But real confession comes from a deep inner conviction that God's Word is true and has been given to you by Him.

FOR FAITH TO BE REAL FAITH it must be grounded in truth - otherwise it's a delusion.

No matter how hard you believe that the rusty old heap will take you round the world, it will always be a rusty old heap. No amount of 'faithing' will turn it into a brand new Bentley.

And if God is a reluctant, impotent healer, no amount of 'faith' or prayer or ministry will make any difference to your condition.

Faith involves believing, confessing and acting upon on the truth of God's willingness and power. It sounds complicated, but the simple heartfelt prayer, 'I ask you, my Lord and healer, to heal my child' can be filled with all the belief and confession and action that's needed.

THE WORD 'CONFESSION' means 'to say the same thing as', so when you confess God's words you're stating that you agree with His words and are 100% 'in line' with them. It's a bit like saying 'Amen' to someone else's prayer and really meaning it.

Speaking is a very important part of faith - it's the outward expression of your inner belief. It evidences your belief, and is one of the ways that you get into line with God's words.

When you confess some of the biblical healing promises of God, you're not trying to make them happen, you're aligning yourself with them – you're pressing the clutch!

When you declare, 'You are the Lord my healer', you're not trying to make a miracle happen; you're expressing your dependence on God's healing nature. You're making contact with the power. You're confessing your faith in much the same way as Blind Bartimaeus calling out to the Lord Jesus in Jericho.

CONFESSION ISN'T A TECHNIQUE, it's a reality. God's Word comes to us in a variety of ways – sometimes through reading the Scriptures; at other times in the stillness of our own listening to God; and often through anointed preaching and prophecy.

When you feel an inner witness that God has spoken, when a verse leaps out at you or a sentence in a sermon registers deeply, it's time to take that word into your spirit and begin to believe it.

There may be no outward evidence of healing, but you know that God has touched you by His Word. That is what you confess, the truth of His Word.

You don't say, 'I'm healed, I'm healed'. Instead, you confess what you've received in your spirit and your belief that it will be yours.

Most Spirit-filled believers spend most of their lives living in the gap between God's 'Let there be' and His 'And it was so'.

To pretend that something is so when it isn't is delusion. To pretend that it won't be because it isn't yet is unbelief. The way of faith is different. It involves keeping on confessing that it will be because God has said that it will be.

And, because He has spoken, it will be.

wait patiently

THE GOSPELS KEEP ON STRESSING that God expects you to persevere in prayer and faith.

Luke 11 gathers together some of Jesus' teaching about prayer for you. It includes His famous story about a man who broke social protocol by boldly visiting a friend at midnight just to ask for three loaves of bread – and who then had to persist in his knocking.

At the end of the parable, Jesus explains that it is through the man's shameless boldness, and his dogged persistence, that he'll receive what he needs.

Jesus immediately applies this. It may not be clear in your Bible that Jesus is asking you for bold persistence, but Luke uses a special Greek tense which is best translated as:

'I say to you, keep on asking and it will be given you; keep on seeking and you will find; keep on knocking and it will be opened to you.

For everyone who keeps on asking receives, and he who keeps on seeking finds, and to him who keeps on knocking it will be opened.'
Luke 11:9-11

Jesus says much the same thing to you in His story about a persistent widow, in Luke 18.

Luke introduces the parable by explaining that Jesus told it 'that men always ought to pray and not lose heart'. And Luke ends the parable with Jesus' question about faith: 'when the Son of Man comes will he really find faith on earth?'.

It's clear from this that true faith and holy persistence are related. Faith does not mean that you ask once for healing and then sit back doing nothing.

Instead, true faith means that you keep on believing, praising and expecting until you receive what God has promised you.

Sometimes this involves keeping on asking the Father, keeping on boldly confessing His words, keeping on reminding Him of His healing promises until the answer comes.

At other times, however, you will need to ask Him only once – for God may give you a strong witness in your spirit that your prayer has been immediately answered.

At these times, you don't keep going by asking, you keep going by praising God for His answer AND by prophetically addressing the 'mountains of opposition' which are blocking you from receiving the answer.

You persist with your praising and addressing until the 'mountains' are flattened and the way is clear for your answer to come. (There's more about speaking to your mountains of opposition in my book 'PRAYER THAT GETS ANSWERS'.)

Whether God leads you to persist in asking or addressing, you can be sure that you'll often need to wait with bold perseverance for healing.

NEVER GIVE IN TO YOUR DOUBTS, even if you can't see any evidence in your body that you're being healed. True faith is bold and persistent faith, and Jesus will not turn you away.

Your heavenly Father knows that it is hard to keep going like this. It's why the Bible says:

'Do not become sluggish, but imitate those who through faith and patience inherit the promises'. *Hebrews 6:12*

Do you see that it doesn't just say 'through faith'? There's no room here for 'easy believism', you need to wait with patience, persisting in your belief, your asking, your confessing and in addressing your obstacles.

Of course, God does sometimes work instantly and immediately. And He does sometimes heal when nobody has asked Him. But you can't presume that He will work like this if you aren't prepared to walk His way.

God is God. You cannot limit Him. But He has made it clear that He expects you to persist. And the experience of Spirit-filled believers through the ages insists that God's healing usually comes after much 'faith and patience'.

If you're serious about receiving healing from the Lord your healer, you will be prepared to wait with patience and will be ready to persist in whatever way He leads you.

DO YOU REMEMBER those television adverts for a certain type of battery? It involved a group of mechanical bunnies playing the drums.

One of the bunnies had the 'longer lasting battery' and this one kept on playing long after all the other bunnies had fallen to the ground.

It was a wonderful picture of faith! When everyone else gives up, and stops believing and confessing, you're going to keep going with true faith – like the bunny with the better battery.

You're going to persist. You're going to persevere through every difficulty, delay and setback. You're going to flatten every obstacle. You're going to get there in the end.

It won't be easy. There'll be times when Satan will tempt you to think that the Lord has abandoned you.

He'll try to discourage you if your healing is very gradual; and he'll urge you to give up when your faith is tested by a setback or some of your symptoms return.

But you're going to persist.

You are, aren't you?

THE BOOK OF HEBREWS contains a special promise about God's faithfulness.

'Let us hold fast the confession of our hope without wavering, for He who promised is faithful.' *Hebrews 10:23*

Your Father isn't an evil parent who gives His children a scorpion when they ask Him for bread. He's a good Father who delights to give good things to His children.

You can trust Him! He is faithful. If you put your confidence in God's Word, you will not be disappointed.

Many believers have to go through a great time of struggle with sickness and difficult family situations. It's part of living in this groaning world. But you mustn't give up.

Lay hold of God. Stand firm on His promises. Keep asking your good Father to act according to His nature. Keep addressing those obstacles. Wait boldly with faith. You will see your reward.

seek verification

IT'S IMPORTANT that you don't claim to be healed if you really haven't been. It doesn't help you and it doesn't honour God.

Genuine healings, real lasting improvements in a medical condition, pass the doctors' tests.

It's especially important that you don't stop taking any prescribed medicines until your doctor says that you can.

It's very irresponsible to throw medicines away just because someone has prayed for you or said something to you. That's not God's way.

God will heal you in His way and His time, and it's presumptuous to throw your medicine away and say, 'Lord heal me'. Very often, it's got nothing to do with faith.

Instead, if you believe that God has healed you, seek proper verification. Visit your doctor and ask him or her to check you out again. Ask them to see what's happened to your condition.

If the doctor says that you don't need the tablets anymore, you haven't wasted the prescription – and you've a wonderful testimony for the doctor.

THERE'S A GOOD CHANCE, however, that your doctor isn't a believer and that he or she won't be impressed by your testimony.

Don't get into an argument with them; just explain that your improvement occurred after asking God to heal you. Most doctors don't know what a miracle is, as they're not trained to recognise them. In fact, it may be better not to use the word miracle – just talk about getting better after prayer or being healed by God.

Even though your doctor may not understand how the change in your condition has occurred, they can tell you whether there has been a change or not – and that's what matters.

Your public testimony is much more credible when you can report that your doctor has examined you and said that you're better.

If you want your unbelieving friends and relatives to trust the love and power of God, it's no good just saying that you're healed. Because of the society we live in, you'll probably need to get some medical evidence that they will trust.

DO YOU REMEMBER the story of the ten lepers who were healed by Jesus? Only one of them went back to thank the Lord. Jesus then instructed the man to show himself to the priest and to make an offering for his cleansing.

Do you see? It was a kind of doctors' check-up. The priests were trained to see whether leprosy was still present and to assess whether or not the leper could return to normal society.

The man couldn't just say he'd been healed; he had to get it verified before the people of his day would believe him and accept him.

So, if Jesus told the healed leper to get his miracle checked by a priest, it's surely not too much for you to visit your doctor.

testify publicly

WHEN YOU HAVE BEEN HEALED it is important that you testify about your healing as a witness to God's power and compassion.

This doesn't mean that you seek to draw attention to yourself. Rather, you should seek to glorify God by your testimony. You may not have an opportunity to testify in front of the whole church. But you could tell at least one or two people what God has done in your life.

Do you remember the story of the naked man who was set free from a legion of unclean spirits? When Jesus cast the spirits into a herd of pigs, the man was restored to his right mind.

This is what Jesus said to the man after he'd been made whole and had put on some clothes.

> 'Go home to your friends, and tell them what great things the Lord has done for you, and how He has had compassion on you.'
> *Mark 5:19*

That's exactly what the man did. Mark reports that, 'He began to proclaim in Decapolis all that Jesus had done for him, and all marvelled'.

YOUR TESTIMONY won't necessarily convert anybody. But it will demonstrate God's concern for the sick, it will point people to the availability of His power, and it will remind them that Jesus is alive.

Remember that God heals you because He loves and cares for individual sick people, and because He is totally opposed to disease and sickness. He heals you because He's concerned about YOU, and not just to advertise His power.

Nevertheless, healing testimonies can make a considerable impact. John 4 reports that a nobleman and all his household believed when the man's son was restored to health by Jesus.

And all the Gospels describe the awe and admiration that ordinary people felt for Jesus when they heard about His healing miracles.

It's the same in Acts. Crowds flocked to the apostles when they heard about the healings.

And much of the early church's rapid growth was due to the people's longing for healing being satisfied by Jesus through the believers.

SOME OF THE HEALING TESTIMONIES in the Gospels, however, had a different sort of impact. At times they led to antagonism and argument, or to opposition and persecution.

For example, the beggar who was healed in John 9 was excommunicated when he testified; and the priests plotted to assassinate Lazarus when he spoke about his healing.

The devil won't like you being healed, and he'll like you speaking about it even less. In many ways, you'll find that the time after the healing is harder than the time before.

This is because the devil will want to rob you of your healing. And if he can't rob you of that, he'll try to rob you of your joy!

Public testimony is a powerful weapon at times like this. It's an important part of the faith process and helps to 'seal' the healing miracle in your life so that the devil cannot snatch it away.

And testifying with a praising, thankful spirit also actively deals with your enemy. God's Word promises that, 'Praise silences the enemy and the avenger'. Satan will try to steal your joy and healing, but your testimony will silence him.

healed to serve

THE FIRST PERSON TO BE HEALED in Mark's Gospel is Simon Peter's mother-in-law – and preachers have been making jokes about it ever since!

She was in bed ill with a fever, so Simon told Jesus about her. Jesus went to the sick woman, took her by the hand, lifted her up, and immediately the fever left her.

That's wonderful, but it's what the mother-in-law did next that is significant for you. Mark 1:31 reports, 'And she served them'.

It was a similar story for the apostle Paul – when he was still called Saul. He was struck blind on the road to Damascus, and God sent the 'unknown' disciple Ananias to minister to him.

Ananias was worried about his instruction, because he knew that Saul had a warrant to arrest all the disciples. But Ananias obeyed God, visited Saul, laid hands on him, and announced that the Lord had sent him so that Saul could receive his sight.

Again, although it's wonderful that God gave Saul his sight straightaway, it's Saul's response which is important for you. Acts 9:20 states, 'Immediately he preached the Christ in the synagogues, that He is the Son of God'.

HAVE YOU SPOTTED THE PRINCIPLE? Saul and Simon's mother-in-law were healed to serve. Their lives did not continue in the same old way after their healing. Instead, they used their new health in the service of their healer.

Their bodily healing was only one part of the miracle; for when Jesus heals, He touches every part of a life – body, mind and spirit.

God wills to heal you, but He doesn't will only to make your arthritis better or your digestion easier. God does will these things, (He's concerned about your every ache and pain and worry!), but He also wills to make you fully whole and completely mature.

THE LORD YOUR HEALER wills to bring health to your body, peace to your mind, strength to your spirit and salvation to your family.

He wills for you to lay hold of your freedom from guilt and self-condemnation, and to know your righteous standing before Him.

He wills to fill you with faith, and to bring you to the measure of the stature of the fullness of

Christ. He wills that you find your place in the body of Christ, and are equipped for the work of service and ministry.

God wills to heal you more fully and completely than you dare hope, and He longs for you to confess His promises, and to lay hold of His healing with faith. He wills all this, and He wills so much more for you too.

Most important of all, God wills that you love Him and serve Him – in discreet ways like Simon Peter's mother-in-law and also in more dynamic ways like the apostle Paul.

YOU'VE MORE OR LESS COME to the end of this little book now. So now it's time for you to start to put what you've learnt into practice.

Before you move on to look up the healing Scriptures on the final few pages, make sure that you've begun to pray for your own healing, and for the healing of your loved ones.

Look to Jesus now for your healing. He is the Anointed. He is the healer. He is the Lord your healer.

You wouldn't doubt Him if He was physically standing right in front of you. Well, He is with you now, He's with you by His Holy Spirit – and He's with you all the time!

Confess the particular promise of God that He's underlined in your spirit while you've been reading this book. Speak it out to God. Then open your hands to the Lord and start to receive your healing.

biblical passages

THERE'S NOT ENOUGH SPACE in this book to set
out all the biblical passages about healing. But it
will do you good to look the following verses up
and read them in the Word.

If you want to develop an intimate relationship
with the Lord your healer, you'll be wise to
become very familiar with this selection of
passages.

Read them regularly. Meditate upon them
often. Apply the stories to your own situation.
Use the prayers to guide your intercessions. And
confess the promises in faith to God.

Healing stories

Genesis 20:1-18
Numbers 12:1-16
1 Kings 17:8-24
2 Kings 5:1-27
2 Kings 20:1-11
Matthew 9:18-26
Luke 8:41-56
Mark 5:25-34
Matthew 9:27-31
Mark 2:2-12
Matthew 8:1-4
Luke 5:12-14
Luke 7:1-10
Mark 1:29-31
Luke 7:11-17
John 9:1-41
Mark 3:1-6
Luke 13:10-17
Luke 17:11-19
Mark 8:22-26
Matthew 20:29-34
Luke 18:35-43
Acts 3:1-10

Genesis 21:1-3
1 Kings 13:1-25
2 Kings 4:8.37
2 Kings 13:20-21
John 4:43-54
Mark 5:22-43
Matthew 9:20-22
Luke 8:43-48
Matthew 9:1-8
Luke 5:17-26
Mark 1:40-45
Matthew 8:5-13
Matthew 8:14-15
Luke 4:38-39
John 5:1-15
Matthew 12:9-14
Luke 6:6-11
Luke 14:1-6
Mark 7:31-37
John 11:1-44
Mark 10:46-52
Luke 22:49-51
Acts 9:8-19

Acts 9:32-35
Acts 14:8-10
Acts 20:7-12

Acts 9:36-43
Acts 14:19-20
Acts 28:7-8

Prayers about healing

1 Samuel 1:10-11
Psalm 41:4
1 Samuel 1:19 - 2:11
Psalm 107:20

Psalm 6:2
Jeremiah 17:14
Psalm 30:2
Psalm 147:3

Promises of healing

Exodus 15:26
Psalm 41:3
Psalm 103:3
Proverbs 3:7-8
Isaiah 19:22
Isaiah 57:18-19
Hosea 6:1
Matthew 10:1
Romans 8:11, 32
2 Timothy 1:7
Hebrews 13:8
3 John 1:2

Psalm 34:19-20
Psalm 91:10-16
Psalm 116:8
Ecclesiastes 3:3
Isaiah 30:26
Jeremiah 30:17
Malachi 4:2
Matthew 11:4-5
1 Thess. 5:23
Hebrews 12:12-13
1 John 3:8
Revelation 22:1-4

If you want to share your personal testimony about God's healing power, or would like some information about Kensington Temple and the London City Church Network, please write to:

Kensington Temple/London City Church
Kensington Park Road
London
W11 3BY
England

If you would like information about other helpful books, tapes and videos, please contact:

Dovewell Mail Order
Kensington Temple
Kensington Park Road
London
W11 3BY
England
Tel: 0800 521631
Fax: 020 7729 7343